# THEIA
# MANIA

*Theia Mania*, copyright, Dallas Athent and Maria Pavlovska, 2016.
All rights reserved.

ISBN: 978-0-9791495-6-6

ASMS BOOKS ARE DISTRIBUTED BY SPD
Small Press Distribution
1341 Seventh Street
Berkeley, CA 94710
1-800-869-7553
orders@spdbooks.org
www.spdbooks.org

ASMS BOOKS CAN ALSO BE PURCHASED AT
www.blacksquareeditions.org
www.hyperallergic.com

TAX DEDUCTIBLE CONTRIBUTIONS TO ASMS CAN BE MADE TO
Off The Park Press, Inc.
972 Sunset Ridge
Bridgewater, NJ 08807
(please make checks payable to Off The Park Press, Inc.)

TO CONTACT THE PRESS, PLEASE WRITE
AntiSentiMental Society
972 Sunset Ridge
Bridgewater, NJ 08807

AntiSentiMental Society is an imprint of: Off The Park Press, Inc.
John Yau – Publisher
Ronna Lebo – Editor
Boni Joi Koelliker – Editor

Cover image by Maria Pavlovska, copyright 2016

Design and composition by Eve Siegel, www.evesiegel.com

# THEIA MANIA

**DALLAS ATHENT** *poetry*
**MARIA PAVLOVSKA** *art*

## Acknowledgements

Dallas:
Thank you Ronna Lebo for being a constant inspiration
in poetry and painting. Thank you Nathaniel Kressen
for being a partner in writing all these years.
Thank you Christian at Nomadic Press for your support.
Thank you Maria for your art.
Thank you Lisa Levy for everything.
Thank you Philippe Avignant for staying true.
Thank you Dom for being my rock.
And thank you to Eve Siegel whose artistic thought
made this book possible.

Maria:
Maria would like to recognize Dallas Athent,
Prospero Vega, and Ronna Lebo.

# DEGENERATE DEITY

i'm drunk in my droptop
    ready to go.
        this skin
            brought to u courtesy of    SEX and CINEMA
              and LET THERE BE LIGHT.
                paste me up within these
                    walls so i am undeniable to u.
                      u *will not*     deny me.
                          u do not see me now but u will see
                        u will see me.

                                                      THE STENCH OF THE SKIN
                                                        comes peeling from ourselves,
                                                          these walls come
                                                               down.      cells cascading
                                                                    to a floor of fat and fauna and
                                                                         now the me u can't ignore.

i am a scumbag goddess.
the girl u see in the night.
the one who walks and fears and drinks.
i am the one that's drunk.

i am a venus rising.
a venus rising from the rain fell to the gutter.
i pick pennies off the ground
and buy keebler wafers from the deli.
here we call them bodegas.
i am a scumbag goddess.

the kind that looks like she might be ok.
the one who surprises you with vodka in a waterbottle.
who let this bitch in the church.

i am the one in the trash.
during your lunch at the office.
i pick at other people's leftovers and the free pretzels.
nothing will ever be wasted.

i am an anonymous girl.
who let her out on her own?
who said that we could walk at night.
the salt is my destination.

everyone at work thinks it's so normal,
on time, under budget, we make it, we
make.
  we make it just work.
    BUT WHAT ABOUT UR LIFE??

    i want to ask
     as i click send on
      the email
       and then think of centuries when
        that could have been a letter,
        and then think i have it good
        and all could be labourious,
         and then think i could be
         huge, lights

w
o
n
d
e
r

w
h
y

i'
m

n
o
t

n
o
t
o
r
i
o
u
s.

we're yankees fans up in the bronx
like YASSSSS
all baseball hats and rough dogs
and success $$$$ MONEy.
did u ever notice how navy just
looks so rich?

walking out the bathroom line. boy rich,
u don't know me! my piss is on the guest list.
tryna put me down in missionary
governor! where is the commissionary?
bring me there if you want me to ride
this *train in vain*. back to earth. *hellloooo*.
looking out of the window of this establishment.
this is entertainment.so get me all jealous
*of lands i'll never see.*

i was actually rich once;
it was england where it
all went down.

(sign of the cross)

my family kept red velvet
on the walls,
grandfather clocks
in the foyer,
the union jack across
our beating hearts.

our bathtubs were raised by
claws.

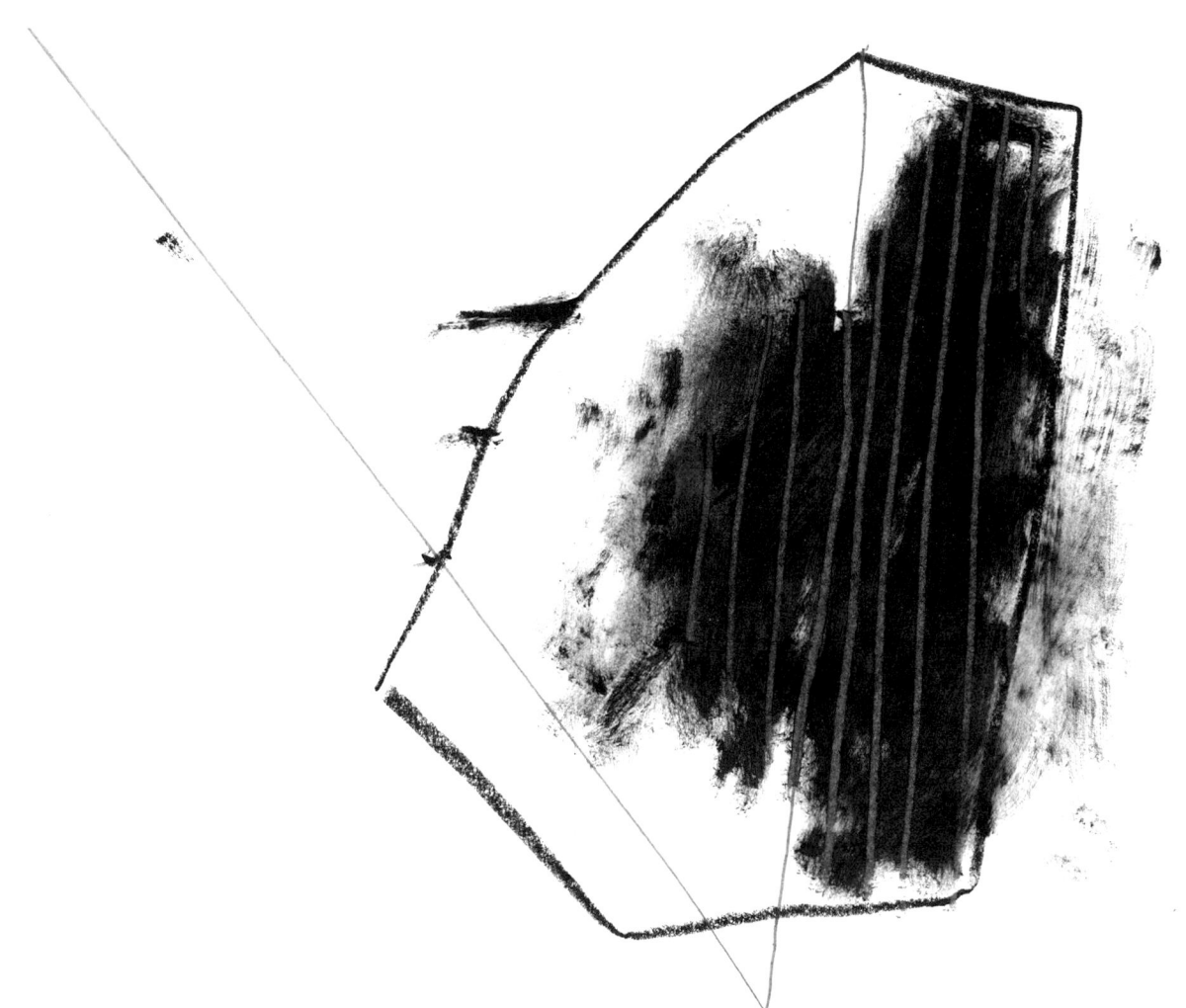

take all of me that u can stand,
 the loud voice and the split ends,
  the cash money falling from
   my ceiling fan
    onto my
     middle class bed,
      and down comforter where
       i take u down with me.

   take the off color remarks
     about how i worked in steerage,
      and what about the empty beer can
       on the nightstand?
        let me know u want it.

       i died when i saw you, worm,
        that pic you took of the girl.
         ur name lookin' like lo mein
          on the blogs and shit.

if it was me in that image
 it would have been better
  cause i know how real old
   money looks old after a
   while and what to do
    to stay new
     for u.

    pride sets in as the drinks wear off,
     i remind myself where i am.
      born to be alone // killing it.
       it's like, the moon is the only moon
        we see.

      soooooo
               every time
                          i see the sky i die.
                                      i die knowing it is there
                                                  and WHATEVER.
                                   there is an oppressive veil separating us from
                                       the stars and yeats. separating us from all that
                                            is holy and whole.knowing and
                                               unknown. all of it i say.
                                                       that it is!

                                   everytime i see the sky i die. everytime
                                   i see u i see the sky, because u are all
                                      i will never know  completely
                                        and i guess i never will.

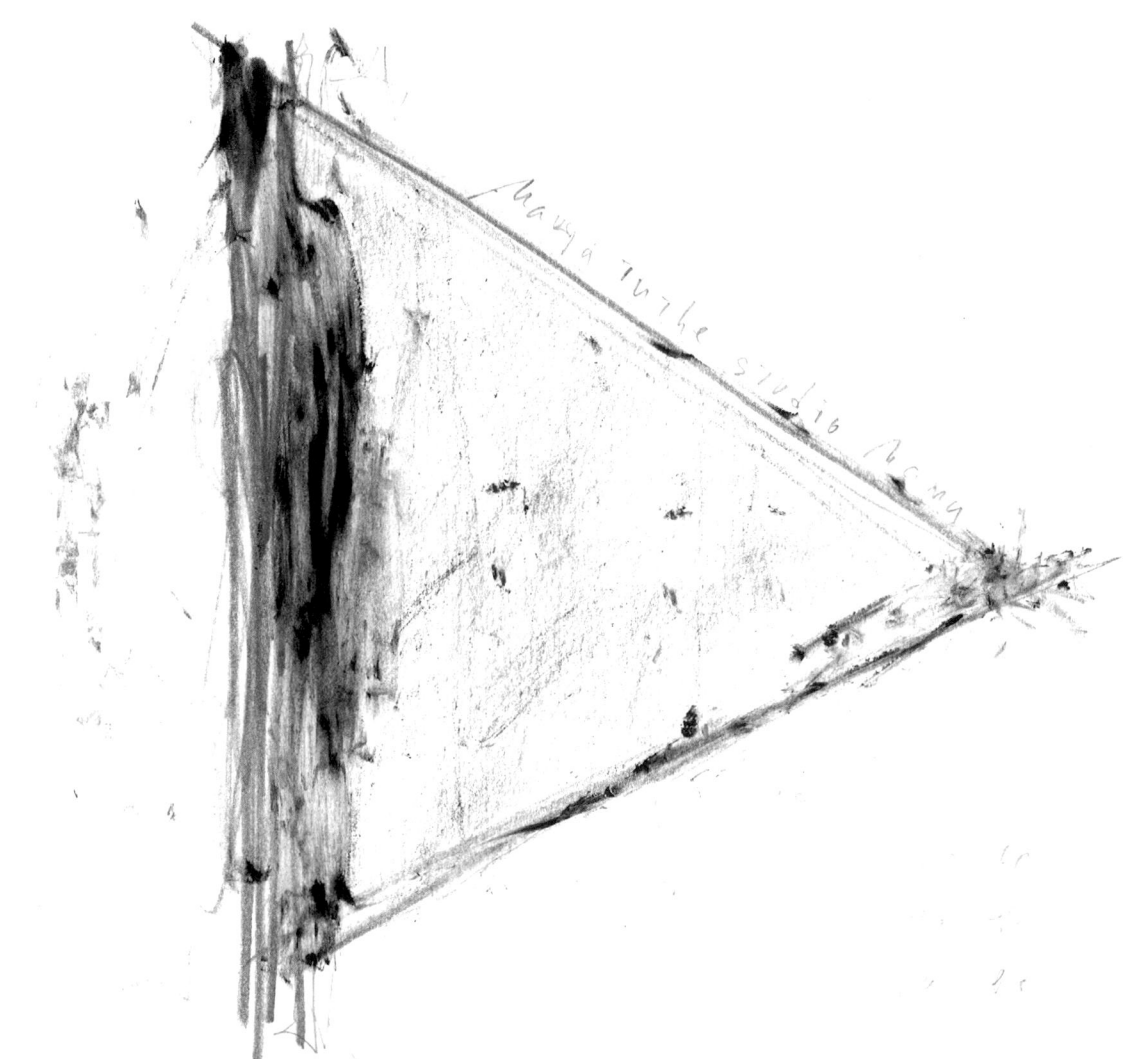

u can't get out of bed.
  smell the corpse.
    that is u on that pillow.
      ur skin. ur cells.
          mortality sets in,
            the sun rising above the window.
              what could u be doing now
                instead?

night's coming now.                the toilet flushes.
u can't avoid it.                    signs of ur body.
so you take to entertainment           you'll just never be
   to avoid it.                          the greatest.

u look out into the distance            scrolling through a feed of
reminded,                                 other people's shit.
in the end at least,                    we have to wonder,
at least we all see the same            who's got it good?
   stars.                         it's 3:24 p.m. and at least hey,
                                    u walked down to the
                                    laundry room.

            ur job isn't the worst.
              but it's not the best either.
                u want something to make u
              feel cool.

dudes hating on em like,
        how dare she be DALLAS.
                how dare she eat a cheese plate,
                        flying buttresses, stones, latte.
                              why won't she
                                  just comfort me
                                        when i made bad choices?

diving deep into this high
        hoping it can change u.
                                          why's she in construction?
u ask me what's up, what's up,
                                                they NEED to
gotta know what's up.
                                                      know.
want me to honest?
                                    how i built a home,
just lay it out all on the line
                                        on my own.
like lingerie in our uptown summer?
                                  it's my land, i regarded it.
show u all the marks you'll reject?
                          deal with it as you form food
                            in ur kitchen, it's possible to eat now.
let me get high on my own.
let me do things on my own.
                            it's like they want a piece of this,
                              stretching me across town like
let me walk these streets, no bag on my arm,
                     i have spandex skin,
no body on my arm,
                  like i got a twin.
             so many versions of me
nothing to tie me to the tracks.
            available to others.
          i know i'm good, i know i'm good.
       bronx baby fire escapes are where i make MAGIC.

        u are palm tree sway,
      a tall looming coconut collection.
   i fell out the tree     on a bed of jasmine all
 stinking fluorescent
and infecting street insects.

i am one.                     crunchy under foot.
     try and step on me // watch me
    splatter all over these damn sidewalks.
     always in ur path and just who are u.
        baby come and talk talk.

so, so capable
so out of nowhere
so out the sky
get it done, get it done
all.

say hello to baseball
bat skyscraper hell.
say hello to the bronx.
say hello to that boy
on the street—
the one with the gold
chain and tshirt.
say hello to ur boss—
let him know you're in
early.
say hello to the
street—
i'll let u in on what u
wanna know.

people have been riding the
PATH train forever. watch me crawl
in a hole. i'm from the mediterranean.
driveway  stone lions are family. i date at
the park and the palace. get drunk in
the comfort of couches. take the train
to you. ask boys out by dropping
a wink. sex and we don't usually do
this. compliment a mom on
her cooking.

buy a
leopard
print
something. develop a crush on his friend.
feel lonely looking at skylines
wish this dinner was from me
to you. blast some good
old sinatra. do be
do be do
be do.

# THEIA MANIA

When he believes that he is safe
tell him the truth,
that he is not safe,
that the fragile parts
of eggs over easy
*are just the first course.*

When he believes that he is loved
let him know what's real,
that he is unloved,

that every meal made
was not by his
mother or a girlfriend.

Then wait for it,
just hold on a sec.
   Have him watch YOU DIE.
Let him know what it is
of you that will never be ignored.
Let him see the decomposing

*of a body that is better*

than anything he will ever know.
The unraveling of the hair, the
finger nails, the lips, the tits.
the pieces of u all over the damn floor,
on for sale at the store, and

everyone is willing to buy,
no matter how good he has it,
they'll STILL give all they got to you.
Because you are not gone.
*You are one hell of a worthy corpse.*

I WANT TO DRINK AT EVERY BAR IN THE WORLD.
I want to drink with all the people of the world, I do!
I want to know them at the pit of it all where
they are their best // worst
and heaven // hell
and dark // light
and starry // night;
which can only be righteously conceived
while drinking.

And so we look for GOD in bars.

This here: this is all the mania I can take.
Sign of the cross and some eggs
on your plate makes you feel alive.
because you're here and I'm here,
and we all need to know our worth.

There's just so many ways to do it.
So many ways to live.

There's headaches for the millions,
for the drinker and sad souls whose
time will make another round like,
we sure care where we are.
Where we call home.

I thought things and told myself I was an artist.
I felt things and thought I was an artist.
I saw my world, my way, called it art.
Threw things up on the wall and let
everyone know I made them.

So this here: this is all the tough love that I can stand.
Do a sign of the cross and a prayer I'll clean up
tomorrow. that I'll decide to be the kind
that does the dishes and shows up on time.
That I'll learn to love the mundane, the mundane
in a beautiful world.

Cause there's just so many ways to do it.
So many ways to live.
So why mess around anymore?

The purpose
of art
is horror.

Somewhere in this world
a man in a first-class suit
is enjoying an ice cream
cone and is innocent.

How adorable.     Whatever.

There is a girl to the side of me
doing the same thing I'm doing.
Only we are not each other.
But she could be my sister.     Whatever.
     Choose me.

But what about the children?
They usually ask this once
I've come around.
But that is not the point now,
is it?

I need you to stop fucking with
me this instant. My heart is at
every train stop for you. Right there.
at the top of the Juliet escalator.

Meet me.
At the cafe.
That way
I can be seen somewhere
sober with you
and know it's real.

Meet me. By the bookshelf.
So we can both read something
dusty but like both understand it.

Cause I'm down, down, baby, baby.
come down here with me.
I know you want to be the one.

big paper...
I'm going through the
paper
and messy foundies
big
mess
mess
mess
voyes

he is
self...
cold
2013 alone
to
mama

So much anxiety.
I can't even swallow.
Everything is a lump.
Everything is a bump
*in the road*.

Just how do u expect me
to sleep tonight?

The terrors, the terrors!
What could happen?
Anything. EVERYTHING.
But let's be honest—
*nothing would be worst of all.*

Threaten a fortress,
don't take what I built.
White rice means the world to me.

I feel powerful and then
powerless.
It's like I own everything
and then not a thing.

This is the downfall of AN ARTIST.
Then I wonder what things do for us
anyway.

Things make us feel like
our life is something to be envied.
Things make us feel like
we have control.
Things make us feel like
we don't need to feel
at all
because
there are
no hOles.

    Drinking in the street.
Don't give a damn.
Light up the night.
      Apologizing for
your damage.

Stars in the night. See myself in the cold.
Walking alone. Pavement's not hard enough.

Dangerous and dark. It's where we live.
This is my hometown. I welcome you all.

Apply again. Don't get a call. Doesn't matter anyway. Nothing is real.

Abducted again. Always eating animals. looking fly as hell. Cry about it later.

Got my nails done. Bought a new skirt.
Got fucked again. Fucked over the world.

Drank all the vodka. Lodged in the summit.
Everything freezes. Wrap it in leaves.

Anonymous girl. Question the world.
Fall on your face. Rise from the earth.

Epic foundation. Rattle the bricks.
Spraypaint the town. Leave names behind.

Grew old too fast. Pissed off the neighbors.
Burned all the incense. Covered the evidence.

Sang to myself. Pizza rat in a cage. Despite all my rage. Thank God for Medicaid.

Hitting people with words. Counting the dollar.
Don't need that many. These streets are us.

Scream!
Silent scream
Scream
big scream...

Aaaa
aaaaa
aaaaaa
aaaaaa

2013, october
9:40pm
leave me alone and my
paper and
pencil
scream!!!!

We drank up all the television images.
Why do we sell ourselves like this?
Love messes. Love money.

Riding the West Coast exploring impossible mountains and their droughts in the comfort of a car courtesy of Tokyo. Turn up the AC up, please.
    Open that bottle of water.

      America lives to be ridiculous.

So really this is US (our story so u know): US GIRLS hang on rooftop bars allowing all the men to buy us all the drinks. Credit card, max it out. There's always more where that comes from
    I swear I swear I swear, but don't swear on me cause we live to be ridiculous.
    WE wear leggings & tank tops to top hat and tails steak dinners.
    More purple eyeshadow. May be a windbreaker.

When I go get a greasy burger I'm in heels and a dress and so, so much eyeliner. It extends all I see and all you see of me.
    I eat the french fries off my friend's plate until she hits me upside the head.
    "Get your own, bitch."

We're all entitled, here. we beg we beg we bed. America.
    GOD.
 OUR SAVIOR BABY JESUS FALLING FROM THE SKY.

There is not a day that passes
that I do not think about death.

How am I gonna do it?
How am I gonna go?

We sit in our skin in a bar
and we talk and we

are friends. Yes, I suppose
that is just what we are.

Someday we **will not be here**
I will go som**ewhere //**
you will go som**ewhere.**

It may be rivers **from  now,**
 years or tomorrow

that I sit and rem**ember the**
time we had drink**ing**

right there----skin on that stool.
Someday we will not be here

**I will go somewhere //**
**you will be someone.**

**But I'll never know completely**
**just what happened to my friend**
**and I guess I never will.**

Pictures of an Atlas
playing baseball with a
semi-automatic weapon and the ball = my <3.

This is what it means to be Atlas.
This is what it means to be Dallas.

The ball is now far out in the distant desert
while you're at home base with your
boys and a beer and you will
always always be death
to me.

I want to thank those who made this possible. My nest egg. This is for you. My money. This is all you.

To every time someone handed me their leftovers. For Ben & Jerry's free cone day. For all the jobs that paid me equally even though I was a woman.

For all the friends and randos and random friends of friends who said "let's take a taxi" and when I suggested the train they said, "It's okay, I got it." For the club promoters who needed a somewhat more than halfway decent looking chick whose eyes light up with 99cent silver eyeshadow in a dark room to sit in and a table and fill the space in exchange for a bottle. You made this happen.

To the frivolous people who drop twenties on the sidewalk. I'm about every office coordinator that got a little too liberal with an executive lunch order and allowed me to lurk around outside a conference room at 2 p.m. to see what was left. To the drunks who bought me a round at the bar. You idiots. I love you.

For the rich families who paid me cash babysitting. For working in England one summer and making money in the Pound and then smiling at the conversion rate. Thank GOD they never adopted the Euro.

Dear banker that waived all of my fees for six months that I didn't realize I was getting charged after the bureaucracy of Chase bank ruled its reigning hand of money falling from the sky suddenly over my measly account. You saved me. Really.

For Boost Mobile's $35 unlimited talk, text and data plan. Who needs an iphone? I own my life. For the friends who didn't call me a scumbag when I carried a flask to the bar. To Rainbow, for being a cheapass never looked this good.

To the IT guy at my old job who never narc'd me out for printing fliers for performances on a mass scale. To people who actually paid me for those performances, even if it was only $10 and a drink ticket. To my friends who hooked it up with retail discounts. 25% off of 40% off of something that's already on sale is basically nothing. For The Met for accepting $1 entry fees to see kick ass art and overall, make me a better person and not a just a regular degenerate roaming these streets.

This is to my neighbor for loaning me a WiFi password and then forgetting. This is for the buybacks because it always helps when you get anything back. This is for my favorite restaurant going on Groupon and CitiBank who tried to ruin my credit in exchange for flier miles. Don't worry fools. Nobody holds down Dallas.

For Piece of Chicken, and Cinderella Falafel, RIP. 99cents can taste gourmet. For Georgi's and being able to put a fake, custom label on a bottle of Vodka and being able to give it out as a gift for 25 cents extra. For the fucking New York Public Library.

Seize my skin, cells wrapped around the bar waiting to be picked up    by      you so no matter which  stool you choose, you choose me.

So many me's, so many pieces of us hangin' around this place.

 I  proactively  came together    once, stitching up the cells so it all  became  something comprehensible:  thread containing       a  me  put together: a version to be admired even if it was just for a moment just to prove it could actually happen    that I could actually do it,                            ya know?

I'll never forget when you snagged the thread that  morning and things came unraveling and everything  got messy. that was so funny, wasn't it LOL! (BTW  I'm   sorry   about   your  throw pillow.)

It's still dark in this bar  where  I'm  no longer a tangible thing       for now.  But that will change. Oh yes it will! Cells bring themselvesbacktogether to become something great    and near.

Behold! This land on which we live. Tell me of its wonder:
of a mourned mouse in the field decomposing among
the brush. Did you craft mortality?

Who knew teeth would always grow on animals. Who
imagined the knolls of these hills and their height
on which the rodentia passed?

Tell us all if it were you.
You, who made every little detail
in such never ending cinema.
But something makes me guess
you just weren't it.

When things said no to you and you were powerless to
change them, just what did you do?
Did you react with reign
or rain?
Or did you sit and wonder

what is earth, even?

Let him see me and know
    *that I am famous*.
        That I will always be paid.
            These riches. This bitch is.
        I churn out colors and get back,
He knows that I AM DALLAS.
      something tangible, *so with it*.
He knows that I AM ATLAS.
        Something to go to hell with.
So there's no starving.
          Something to rent a motel with.
berries all over my bed.
Grease all over his head like,
a man yells in the forest
and the animals hear it
              SO THE QUESTION IS
but if he yells at his wife
          if you see less of me,
in the comfort of home
       will you love more of me?
well, does anyone hear that?
      If I don't hit you back,
        will you hit me up?
     If you wonder where I am,
Stay still // I will
    if I post less to the world,
I am. The one.
  if I starve myself to nothing,
Who draws.
  well, *just how are you gonna handle all that*?
    But he calls, and calls me what I am.
      Of course he does.

Girls are so much better behaved than boys. It's hard to believe that we're actually the same. The only thing that separates us is the size of our tits and shit.

The child to the left of me did what she had to do. Took her phone, put it inside airplane mode. I mean the steward-ass only made the announcement once and she had already done it. In fact, the girl in front of me put her blinker on well in advance just in    case. What a nice thing to do! To be considerate of others and all.

So what's up with this world? I'll tell you a secret. I'm drunk with a shock top in a parking lot, sucking all the cigarettes, looking at the moon like a fucking wolf. Looking at men like I was raised by wolves. I don't belong with the boys, though. I'm just not that cool. It's because of all of the violence.

But with the animals I am free. We sex we sleep we eat.
Lather rinse repeat.

She joined the wet t-shirt contest
to feel her breasts had the power to be
immortal.

TO JUST FEEL LIKE
maybe for once, all eyes were on her.

That her beauty  defied    THE GODS
and wasn't created
by     something she had
nothing to do with, really.

And that even after the bar had closed all of the people would remember: she was the winner. Yep. She was belle of the ball.

I do what I want because
I AM the venus rising
from the glow of a   burnt-down bodega
(or perhaps, a busted-up bar).

He is what he is because
HE IS the Atlas rising
from the ashes of a   burnt-out sun
(or, ya know, here comes the sun king).

We die when we die because
WE ARE the phoenix rising from the cells
of this   earth and all of heaven and hell
that can be found
theirin.

Touring life of the rich
in diamonds and decanters.
I don't belong here.
I so belong here.
I can go anywhere.
*Just watch me fucking nail it.*

Watch me flourish in money
you did you didn't idk.

Watch me watch what's mine.
What I make, it all is here.
These trees are my hands,
this cocktail is my fucking power.

Beauty at 90
this work was refined
but ya'll don't know
*stars yawn.*
You'll fade to a state
hold your gun then,
aim to what you
*can't nail.*

I'm a 60s babe
70s frame.
Born in the 80's..
live sick filming 80s.

When I do, I'll do good,
when I weekend
people will listen,
and when I own
you will know of
*my animals.*

Every salty grain the English dreamed
and dissolved into their regions.
Know the powers of the channel
and the blood that washed with it.

We bare crosses
and hold up shields so comically.
It's all we ever talk about.
our messes, our money.

Honestly, I think it's tacky the way we
roll around town like--
hey it's my chips, I'm rich
and us being all classy-nasty like
is what I like about it.

Just be honest.
Just be honest.
Just ask yourself this very important question:
When you are walking in old timey things,
in places that know bones and disease,
in places that know more about you than you do,
just who are you to the rest of the world?

Everything.
Nothing.
Things and then not things.
Matter and then you don't matter anymore.

So here is what I learned in London:
everything isn't money and property,
Oh  no no no no no!
Although that certainly helps
move things along--ya feel me? (winks)
Everything is love and love and attitude
and maybe even
a little bit of attention.

SO I go to England. Where I belong. I see the gray and brick and towers of mirth and gloom. I feel the powers of nations rolling on history and the river Thames, bones washed ashore and discarded. And I feel rich. Richer than a Sulton. There are clocks that could have paid for my college. There are canes with marble balls for handles that only a diplomat could be seen with. We're so drunk, Tascha and I. My spirit: Tascha. The mother of this earth and then some: Tascha. Project Venus: Tascha. A woman who laughs at her own socks: Tascha. We had all the wine in the world. All the wine on the table. And then we had cheese.

"those were dark days."
"those were dark days."
those were dark days,
we speak of Wolverhampton.

And they were,
They were.
They were eating-beans-
from-the-can-dark, love-on
-a-dollar-dark, hide-from-the-
conductor-dark, give-your-last-
dime-to-a-friend-dark.
No one ever knows.
Then my heart hurts.
Where's Sal?

I call out to him.
Let the spirits know--
he should know,
he should be here, he should be here.
But he's not here. He never will be.
He'll never fucking get it.

So Tascha and I day-drink, walking about Shoreditch and eating overpriced sandwiches with things like cranberry and brie on them. Then we pound down the Guinness over talking with old English men and play pool and everyone loses and nobody's a winner in this town. We make no new friends. We make no new enemies.

Then my heart hurts.
Where's Sal? Where's Sal?
I say, I cry.

You and me Sal:
Walking along the River Thames with the bones.
You and me Sal:
Drinking in the pub, lighting up the night.
You and me Sal:
Eating bread with salted ham on it.
You and me Sal:
Seeing art we'll never pay for.
You and me Sal:
Wondering if we'll ever afford this velvet.
You and me Sal:
Drinking tea between bricks in the rain.

Some things you cannot explain how rich they are.

Playing pool and day drinking and wearing bad makeup is so, so rich.

Being in the darkness with the velvet and must and books and friends is so, so rich.

Loving a man so much it hurts when he's across an ocean is so, so rich.

Tascha and I were always Venuses. We were always rich.

Even with hurting hearts.
Even in Wolverhampton.

"those were dark days."
"those were dark days."
those were dark days.

Pain is some thing we'll always know.

LIFE IS LIKE
a box of screenshots.
You never know what
people are going to
repost and regret.

#social #media

Ya feel me?

What will be
remembered?
What will stick
around like the
Russian dolls a
grandma gave you?

All of it sticks. The tits.
The dicks. The shit.

I guess
we have
no soul.

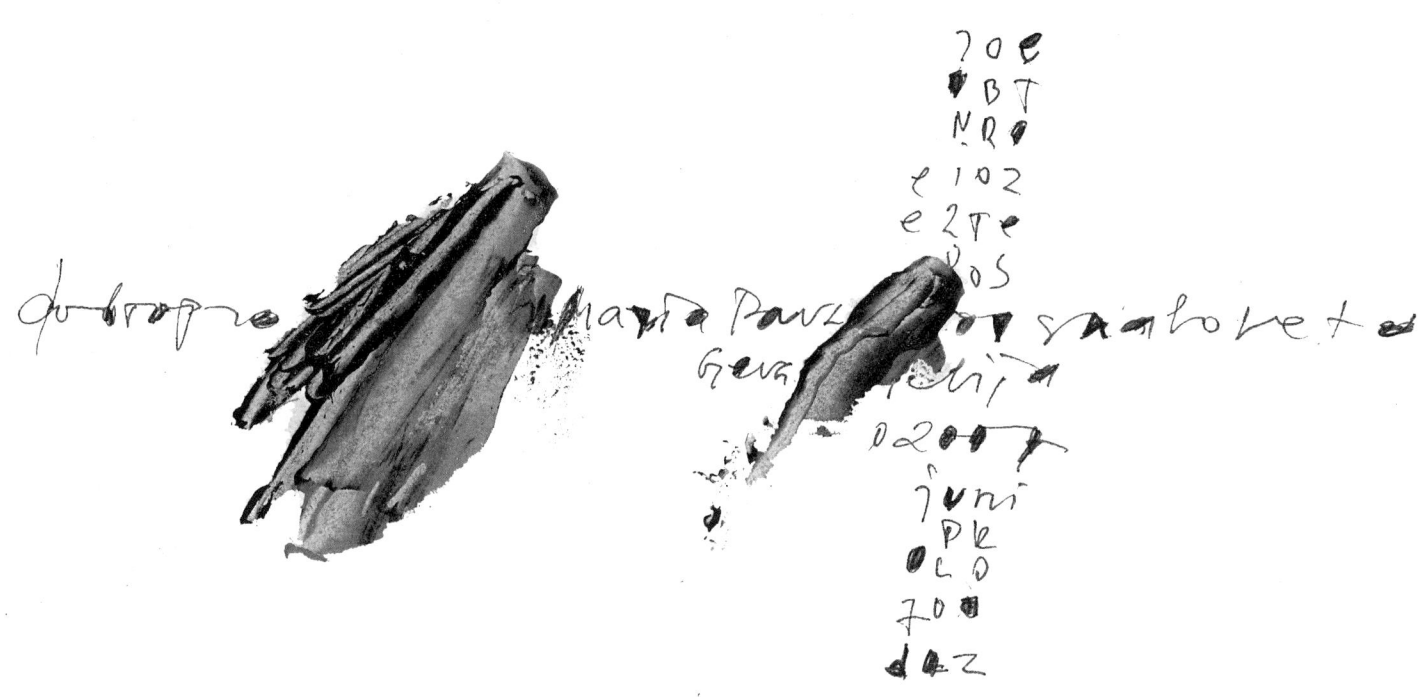

                              to take all of this?
                            The plight of the artist.
                            Who can do justice to
                               the suffering.

Can I be drunk enough    Cause someone has to do it.          All of us together,
                          Someone has to make things,          people make so
                          and how do you even know                  many
                             what's good anymore?

                         I'm making use of
                          you right now,
                         your piles of shit.
                       Watch my hand be a wand.
                       Watch this bitch be a witch.

 

mistakes and then some.
They were gonna buy buy
barely, they didn't.
But at least it works.
It never works.

When bae gets laid off
I feel for him.
When we sleep
I feel for him.     What is missing even?
When he coughs
unable to sleep
cause of his culture
of Carhartt and pain,
oh, I feel it.
But when I cheat on hearts
and dream on stars
I feel for me.

What could make it better?
What is missing even?

tassionisc&lve

golemisibipomo

onvaivadvajcata

spiviaostdeshi

Say hello to baseball bat skyscraper tall broken down bricks, weeds that tell you they're your neighbor like hellloooooo. The old Stella Dora is no longer door to doora. Those were the good bad old dayz. An empty armory and the cities up in arms about it. Wasting time on the vine up the fire escape hell. You say pizza in a basement is down and everybody's getting high in this city. Divided we are. Divided by water divided by highways divided by hearts. Burn it up and we're together again in this fire. The rest of NYC will never ever get it. Moses is known for separating seas and now separating families. Watch how this bad bitch popping dirt bike on the Cross Bronx just to make a point. Just to prove a girl could do it ya know?

An Edgar Allen Poe relic, still standing on a porch just as doomed as the bones he wrote into their walls. Cross to Yonkers and you have the claddagh come down on you hard. Chess on a sidewalk plan your moves or forget your bet, you're never getting a cannoli. White Plains road is actually colorful fabric flowing Ankara all over these damn windows. Attachment issues, attached to the mainland so screw you special snowflake island boroughs. Save us your complexes. Orchard Beach in a half moon milking moms of their Sundays, kids playing in polluted channel but hey, it's something. The zoo is the heart of it all because we are all animals in broken down brick walls with our own pride, with our own stripes and spots. Ride over to Riverdale see sweeping villas swallowing palisades rolling rocks foundations for what Rockefeller built. You get it? Rich people live here. We gather together pub TV watching Sundays radio listening internet checking stadium sitting to survey our team. The emblem of NYC. Ride the Triboro out of another borough and cross the line. You'll see it there. Welcome to THE BRONX baby. We've been waiting for you.

I said no when they told me
I'd need them,

lions on my shoulders.

They did not listen.
They tried to mess around.
Tried to hold me down.

I told them,

There's a girl to the side of me
doing the same thing I'm doing,
but we are not each other,
instead she is my sister.
It doesn't matter. Choose me.

WE ARE: minding our split ends trimming one by one
WE ARE: carrying drugs for him in the rucksack
WE ARE: deciding between a drink and a cupcake
WE ARE: choosing the perfect shade of pink
WE ARE: debating getting that blouse at the store
WE ARE: wondering should we pregnancy or YOLO
WE ARE: eating tuna fish salad at a cafe
WE ARE: switching from flats to heels and geisha
WE ARE: switching back to flats after the heels prove too cumbersome
WE ARE: kicking ourselves for forgetting the tampons
WE ARE: crying because he hurt our friend and we love her
WE ARE: telling ourselves we're better off on our own
WE ARE: installing and uninstalling dating apps
WE ARE: biting our nails at work and then getting them done
WE ARE: pulling our knees in on the subway
WE ARE: leaving names behind in the stalls

So yes we are sisters, but don't think
because we are, we are one.
Not so easy,
and don't try to hold down DALLAS,
because whatever we are doing
I have lions on my shoulders. I told you.
I'm my only self. I am everything.